To Douglas,

Your very own book! All about you!
All about how God cares for
you and loves you and
how thrilled your mum and
Dad are that you are part
of their family.

from Catherine

May The Lord bless you and keep you
May The Lord make his face to shine upon you
and be gracious unto you.
May The Lord lift up his face towards you
and give you peace.

Our Baby Book

Illustrated by Karen Buckle
Text by Carine Mackenzie

Published by
Christian Focus Publications Ltd.

Geanies House, Fearn,
Tain, Ross-shire, Scotland, IV20 1TW

ISBN 1-85792-026-0
© Christian Focus Publications 1993

Text by Carine Mackenzie
Designed by Donna Macleod
Illustrated by Karen Buckle

Contents

Weight _____ 7 pounds and 14 ounces. _____ 20
Height _____ 21
Progress _____ 22
Favourite Food _____ Breast milk. _____ 24
Favourite Toys _____ teddy daddy bought me. 25
Health Record _____ All is well. _____ 26
Illnesses _____ none. _____ 27
First Outings To Gangans house for dinner. 28
Photos _____ At Gangans _____ 29
First Holidays _____ 30
Photos _____ 31
Special Friends Anna Piepe _____ 32
Photos _____ 33
Going to Sunday School St Andrews. Hertford. 34
Photos _____ 35

Birth Day

I will praise you because I am fearfully and wonderfully made

Psalm 139 v14.

name _Douglas Alexander Micheal Yannaghas._

date _2nd August 1997._

place _Queen Elizabeth II Hospital, Welwyn Garden City._

time _8am._

weight _7 lbs and 14 ounces._

length _____

eyes _blue._

hair _golden blond._

5

First Photos

From my birth I have relied on you

Psalm 71 v6.

Announcements
I bring you good news of great joy

Luke 2 v10.

Telegraph

Northern Times.

7

Visitors

Love each other as I have loved you

John 15 v12.

Betty King Caroline Yannaghas Anthony Yannaghas
Roberta Allison   Sandra Macdonald.

Congratulations Received

Elizabeth gave birth to a son. Her neighbours and relatives shared her joy

Luke 1 v57.

Phone-calls Received

Presents Received

Every good and perfect gift is from above

James 1 v17.

Family Tree

One generation will commend your works to another; they will tell of your mighty acts

Psalm 145 v4.

Micheal Yannaghas
grandfather

Caroline Yannaghas
grandmother

Anthony Yannaghas
Tobby Dougie Mackay
ndia Lachie Mackdonald
ven Deo Munro.
aunts / uncles
Shona Allison
erdm Scott Cowan.

Cousins,
Lewis Mackay, Chris Mackay,
Laclan Macdonald Ryle Macdonald
Dean Munro
Stuart Allison Ian Allison
Fiona Cowan, Scott Cowan.
other relatives

13

Daily Routine

Every day I will praise you and extol your name for ever and ever

Psalm 145 v2.

Breakfast 8am

lunch 12-1pm

Dinner. 5-6pm

Snacks and drinks when required

Sleeping Habits

When you lie down
your sleep will be sweet

Proverbs 3 v24.

first sleep through night _____

_____

_____

_____

day time nap after lunch. _____

_____

_____

_____

bed time _____

_____

_____

_____

_____

First Visit to Church

From infancy you have known the Holy Scriptures which are able to make you wise for salvation through faith in Christ Jesus.

2 Timothy 3 v15.

date _____ _____

church St Andrews Church Hertford. England.

minister Reverend Graham Edwards

christening December 14th 1997.

baptism December 14th 1997.

dedication _____

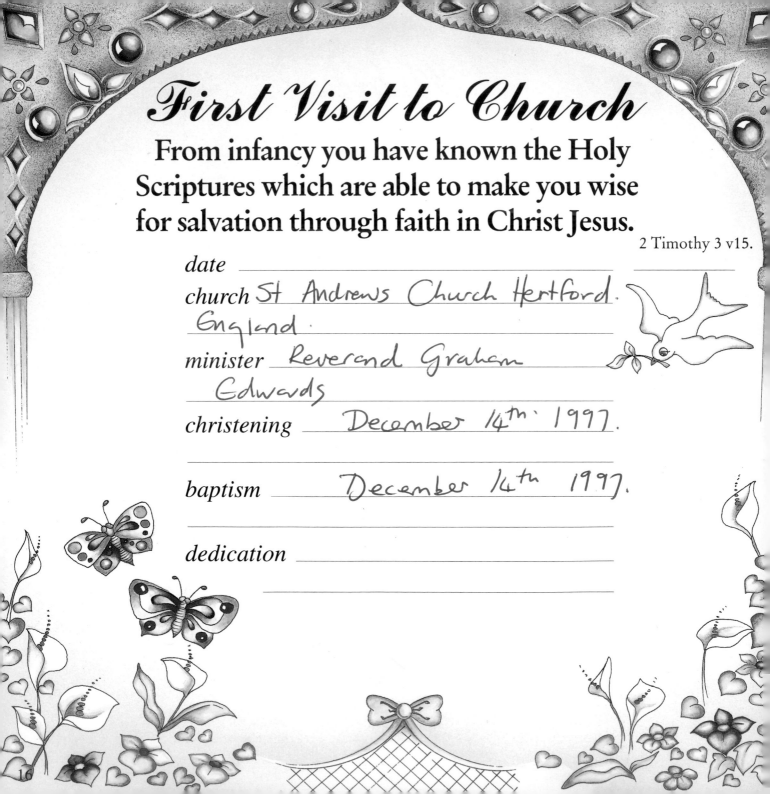

Photos

Good Looks

Even the very hairs of your head are all numbered

Matthew 10 v30.

lock of hair   *hand print*   *foot print*

Teeth

The child grew and became strong   Luke 2 v40.

first tooth _____

_____

second tooth _____

others ___7 teeth Aged 9 months.___

all teeth _____

_____

19

Weight

Jesus grew in wisdom and stature and in favour with God and men

Luke 2 v52.

birth _____

2 weeks _____

4 weeks _____   1 year _____

2 months _____   2 years _____

3 months _____

4 months _____   3 years _____

5 months _____   4 years _____

6 months _____

9 months _____   5 years _____

Height

birth _____

2 weeks _____

4 weeks _____

2 months _____

3 months _____

4 months _____

5 months _____

6 months _____

9 months _____

1 year _____

2 years _____

3 years _____

4 years _____

5 years _____

Progress

Let the little children come to me and do not hinder them for the kingdom of heaven belongs to such as these

Matthew 19 v14.

first smile _____

first laugh _____

sitting up Seven and a half months.

crawl 8 months.

step _____

walking _____

Progress

When I was a child I talked like a child

1 Corinthians 13 v11.

first words   Dada . Mama Boo Hello.

first phrases

23

Favourite Food

Like new born babies, crave pure spiritual milk so that by it you may grow up in your salvation 1 Peter 2 v2.

1-4 months egg custard, Rice & milk, Milk, Apple Juice,

4-8 months Strawberry & cream desert, chicken & sweetcorn, Creamed porridge, cheese & veg, bean + bacon, fruit puree

8-12 months Baby Yoghurt, Sunshine Orange, Pasta & cheese, Bolognaise,

12-18 months _____

feeding without help _____

_____

_____

Favourite Toys

The city streets will be filled with boys and girls playing there

Zechariah 8 v5.

favourite toys: <u>Peter rabbit , Mischief teddy , star with teethers, hippopatomus</u>
white teddy; cream rabbit,

6 months <u>Activity cube, books,</u>

1 year _____

18 months _____

2 years _____

playmates _____

25

Health Record

I pray that you may enjoy good health

3 John v2.

clinic visits _____

innoculations _____

Illness

The power of the Lord was present for him to heal the sick

Luke 5 v17.

_____

_____

_____

_____

_____

_____

_____

_____

First Outings

The Lord will watch over your coming and going

Psalm 121 v8.

where _____

when _____

with _____

where _____

when _____

with _____

Photos

First Holidays

You will be blessed when you come in and blessed when you go out

Deuteronomy 28 v6.

where   Lairg Sutherland Scotland

when

memories

where   Edinburgh Scotland.

when

memories

Photos

Special Friends

A friend loves at all times

Proverbs 17 v17.

friend <u>Anna Piepe</u>

where we met <u>across from my house, she lved across the street from me.</u>

friend <u>Lydia Bancroft</u>

where we met <u>At Bible Study on Thursdays when I'm in creche with Lydia.</u>

friend <u>Rebecca Carlow</u>

where we met <u>At Bible Study Creche.</u>

friend <u>Kirsten Ibbetson</u>

where we met <u>My mum is friends with hers as she is a nurse also.</u>

Photos

Sunday School

Train a child in the way he should go and when he is old he will not turn from it.

Proverbs 22 v6.

church St Andrews, Hetford.

date _____

what did I do? Pray with Toys, read stories

Photos

Photos

Photos

Photos

Photos

Photos